A Year of Inspiration

Neville Goddard Quotations

Compiled by
Sharla Race

A Year of Inspiration:
Neville Goddard Quotations

First paperback edition
Published 2014
ISBN: 978-1907119323

Publisher: Tigmor Books
www.tigmorbooks.co.uk

This very day start your new life. Approach every experience in a new frame of mind—with a new state of consciousness. Assume the noblest and the best for yourself in every respect and continue therein.

Neville

Welcome

Neville Goddard was one of the most inspiring Law of Attraction teachers of the twentieth century.

His books are still read today and we are fortunate that some audio recordings also remain enabling us to hear Neville's message as he originally taught it.

The essence of his message—that like attracts like, that we are responsible for everything that happens to us, is a message that cannot change because it is, as Neville says, the Law.

The quotations in this collection come from Neville's books and lecture transcripts. I have allocated one for each day of the year but you are welcome to read them in any order, at random, or all at once!

I hope you enjoy them and find them inspiring. May you always think good thoughts for yourself and for others.

I wish you *every* happiness.

Sharla Race

January

Whatever the mind of man can imagine
man can realize.

1 January

If there were dreams to sell, what would you buy?

2 January

We can be to others only that which we are to ourselves.

3 January

You can remove the seemingly mountainous obstacles which confront you by simply ignoring them and assuming the end. And if you have to go over the mountain, you will, or the mountain will be removed.

January 4

We can determine where we will go by controlling and directing our inner talking.

January 5

If you are ever in doubt always do the loving thing. Then you will know you are doing the right thing.

January 6

We all have one state in which we are very comfortable, so we return to it moment after moment. That state constitutes our dwelling place. If it is not a pleasant state, we can always get out of it.

7 January

To be conscious of being poor while praying for riches is to be rewarded with that which you are conscious of being, namely, poverty.

8 January

We have no one to change but self.

9 January

May I tell you, you have everything it takes to be the man, to be the woman, you want to be? Don't pass the buck.

January 10

If your inner conversations are not what they should be, change them.

January 11

If you spend the day thinking from a certain base, a certain body of beliefs, the chances are you will fall asleep that night in the same belief.

January 12

Do not postpone your dreams and do not think that because you heard what to do, your desires will come to pass. It's so easy to hear the truth and postpone the doing.

13 January

Your world in its every detail is your consciousness objectified.

14 January

Nothing stands between you and the fulfilment of your dreams but facts and facts are the creations of imagining. If you change your imagining, you will change the facts.

15 January

Consciousness is the one and only reality.

January 16

The journey is in yourself.

January 17

As soon as you believe in the truth of the state affirmed, results follow.

January 18

Always hear and accept as true of others that which you would desire for yourself. In so doing you are building heaven on earth.

19 January

You are limited only by your uncontrolled imagination and lack of attention to the feeling of your wish fulfilled.

20 January

You can start now from scratch and choose the being you want to be.

21 January

Many people tell me they cannot meditate. This seems to me a bit like saying they cannot play the piano after one attempt. Meditation, as in every art or expression, requires constant practice for perfect results.

January 22

You cannot change your thinking until you change your feeling, and all feelings come from ideas.

January 23

There is no one else like you and you cannot be replaced in the kingdom of God.

January 24

All that is asked of you is to accept your desire. If you dare claim it, you will express it.

25 January

The most remarkable feature of man's future is its flexibility.

26 January

What is now proved in this world was once only imagined. This is the greatest of all secrets, the secret of imagining.

27 January

When you set out to master the movements of attention it is then you realize how little control you exercise over your imagination and how much is dominated by sensory impressions and by a drifting on the tides of idle moods.

January 28

Never visualize yourself at a distant point in time and space. Make your action take place here and now!

January 29

Personal success will prove far more convincing than all the books that could be written on the subject.

January 30

Man should daily relive the day as he wished he had lived it.

31 January

You don't have to remain in a state if you have made a mistake. You can change states morning, noon, and night, but the state to which you most constantly return constitutes your dwelling place.

February

Faith is believing what is unbelievable.

1 February

You are what you are, so everything is as it is.

2 February

The world cannot change until you change your conception of it.

3 February

Learn to control your own wonderful human imagination. When you do, you will have heaven on earth.

February 4

One must start with oneself. It is one's attitude that must be changed.

February 5

Take no thought of tomorrow; tomorrow's expressions are determined by today's impressions.

February 6

You imagined yourself into your present state. If you don't like it, you must imagine yourself out of it and into another.

7 February

We all regard feelings far too much as effects, and not sufficiently as causes of the events of the day.

8 February

You can open the doors of any prison—the prison of illness or poverty or of a humdrum existence.

9 February

The moment you contemplate an act, it has been committed. Whether it is pleasant and you may be inclined to do it physically, or you restrain the impulse to act upon that which you are contemplating, the act is already done!

February 10

Don't blame; only resolve.

February 11

You are free to choose the concept you will accept of yourself. Therefore, you possess the power of *intervention*, the power which enables you to alter the course of your future.

February 12

When we break a habit, our desire to break it is greater than our desire to continue the habit.

13 February

There is no limit to your creative power.

14 February

Whatever is necessary to be removed for you to fulfil what you have assumed, will be done for you as long as you remain faithful to yourself, the source of all life.

15 February

Events happen because comparatively stable imaginal activities created them, and they continue in being by virtue of the support they receive from such imaginal activities.

February 16

Man's assumptions which he regards as insignificant produce effects that are considerable; therefore man should revise his estimate of an assumption, and recognize its creative power.

February 17

Your awareness is the master magician who conjures all things by being that which he would conjure.

February 18

You can catch a mood and create a world that is in harmony with it. Anyone can do it; in fact, you are doing it morning, noon and night.

19 February

You don't need to hurt anyone to gain anything in this world.

20 February

Your illusion of free will is but ignorance of the causes which make you act.

21 February

When man finally identifies himself with his Imagination rather than his senses, he has at long last discovered the core of reality.

February 22

There is not a problem that cannot be resolved by a change of consciousness.

February 23

Believe that all things are possible to you and that you are what you want to be. Persist in that assumption and it will harden into fact.

February 24

To change a man, you must change your conception of him.

25 February

By feeling your wish fulfilled and quietly relaxing into sleep, you cast yourself in a star role to be played on earth tomorrow and, while asleep, you are rehearsed and instructed in your part.

26 February

Let no man tell you that you should not have your desire. What you feel that you have, you will have.

27 February

What we are conscious of is constructed out of what we are not conscious of.

February 28

If you will not imagine yourself as other than what you are, then you remain as you are.

(February 29)

Some call it imagination, and others call it God.

March

The game of life is played on the playing field of the mind.

1 March

The world, and all within it, is man's conditioned consciousness objectified.

2 March

It is necessary to have an aim in life. Without an aim we drift.

3 March

If you want something, it is not going to come into being by saying: "I will have it someday". That is deferring your hope and making your heart sick.

March 4

Everything in this world needs man as the agent to express it. Hate or love, joy or sorrow, all things require man to express it.

March 5

Use the law and it will take you from success to success, as you conceive success to be.

March 6

Change your conception of yourself and you will, without the aid of masters or anyone else, automatically transform your world to conform to your changed conception of yourself.

7 March

The most horrible problem will be resolved if you will but conceive a solution in your mind's eye. Anyone can do it. It doesn't take an Einstein to imagine a problem is resolved.

8 March

"I will be" is a confession that "I am not".

9 March

All things exist in the human imagination but I need not call them into being.

March 10

There is no fiction.

March 11

Change the image, and thereby change the fact.

March 12

Your life expresses one thing, and one thing only, your state of consciousness. Everything is dependent on that.

13 March

Your consciousness is the cause of your world.

14 March

Live your life fully while here, but remember you can't take your money with you.

15 March

Choose a scene which would imply you already have achieved success and when it unfolds, you will know how it came about. Do this, and you are testing the infinite power that you really are.

March 16

It is the height of folly to expect security while being conscious of insecurity. On the other hand, you cannot be insecure if you walk conscious of being secure.

March 17

You are not the mask you are wearing, you are God.

March 18

No matter what we do, we follow the desire which at the moment dominates our minds.

19 March

Nothing is impossible to imagine, and nothing is impossible to Imagination. Every desire will be yours if you will but dare to assume the feeling that your wish is fulfilled as you go to sleep.

20 March

Health, wealth, beauty, and genius are not created; they are only manifested by the arrangement of your mind—that is, by your concept of yourself.

21 March

Compare what you want with what you have. If they differ you must make the effort to move. You must learn the secret of motion.

March 22

The only thing that prevents us from making a successful subjective impression on one at a great distance, or transforming there into here, is our habit of regarding space as an obstacle.

March 23

What is now proved to be true as far as we are concerned was once only imagined.

March 24

What do you want? Name it and rearrange the structure of your mind to imply you no longer desire it, because you already have it!

25 March

Having assumed the life you now live, no one can take it from you but yourself! You have the power to lay it down by no longer being conscious of it, and the power to pick it up again through consciousness.

26 March

This world, which we think so solidly real, is a shadow out of which and beyond which we may at any time pass.

27 March

To change the world, you must first change your conception of it.

March 28

When you resist evil, you give it your attention, you continue to make it real. When you renounce evil, you take your attention from it and give your attention to what you want.

March 29

Millions of payers are daily unanswered because man prays to a God who does not exist. Praying, then, is recognizing yourself to be that which you desire to be rather than begging God for that which you desire.

March 30

Free will is freedom of choice.

31 March

If you want something don't ask yourself if you are qualified, but if your request is genuine. Do not concern yourself as to how and when it will happen, simply assume that you are there already and, in a way that no one knows, it will take place

April

Leave the world alone and change your
conceptions of yourself.

1 April

Don't be anxious or concerned as to results. Results will follow just as surely as day follows night.

2 April

Moods are not only the result of the conditions of our life; they are also the causes of those conditions.

3 April

Everyone is free to choose the state he wishes to occupy.

April 4

The cornerstone on which all things are based is man's concept of himself.

April 5

All you can possibly need or desire is already yours. You need no helper to give it to you; it is yours now.

April 6

Through imagination man escapes from the limitation of the senses and the bondage of reason.

7 April

That which you do not claim as true of yourself, cannot be realized by you.

8 April

You have the power to create and uncreate. Having brought something unlovely into your world, you can uncreate it if you are willing to create something in its place and persist until your desire becomes fulfilled.

9 April

Imagining the wish fulfilled is the seeking that finds, the asking that receives, the knocking to which is opened.

April 10

You make the choice. You can choose life or death.

April 11

I am not trying to flatter you when I tell you that you are God. Everyone is.

April 12

Rebirth is the dropping of that level with which you are dissatisfied and rising to that level of consciousness which you desire to express and possess.

13 April

You have nothing to do but convince yourself of the truth of that which you desire to see manifested.

14 April

Consciousness is the cause as well as the substance of the entire world.

15 April

Remember: you don't have to abide by anything you dislike. It is but a vessel in your hand which is not properly shaped. Go down to the potter's house and rework it into another vessel.

April 16

We are walking tracks and the tracks are forever, and by the mere curvature of time your next life is this life. You simply replay it; so if you are not proud of it, start now and change your life today.

April 17

Leave the state containing poverty and move into the state containing wealth, and wealth will take on reality.

April 18

Your inward conversations are the breeding ground of all your future action.

19 April

Your future is best changed when you control your thoughts while in a state akin to sleep, for then effort is reduced to its minimum. In that state your attention is relaxed, yet controlled within the feeling without being forced or using effort.

20 April

Two things cannot occupy a given place at one and the same time, and so as the invisible is made visible, the former visible state vanishes.

21 April

Wake from the sleep that tells you the outer world is the cause of the conditions of your life.

April 22

The world cannot tell you anything other than what you are telling yourself.

April 23

Dare to assume you are exactly *what* you want to be, dare to assume you are *where* you want to be, even though your reason and your senses deny it. If you do it, will it work? It doesn't cost you a penny to try it.

April 24

Never accept as true of others what you would not want to be true of you.

25 April

We illuminate or darken our lives by the concepts we hold of ourselves.

26 April

You do not have to limit your power of belief to what your reasonable mind dictates. The choice and its limitations are entirely up to you, for all things exist in the human imagination and it is from your imagination that your belief stems

27 April

You and your world are *one*.

April 28

It is difficult to accept the concept that the world is bearing witness to your thoughts, but it is true. If you do not like something or someone, do not look at it or them; look within to the one who is causing the image

April 29

If you hear something that is unlovely, don't accept it, but instantly revise it. Hear the words that ought to have been spoken and persuade yourself, to the best of your ability, that it is so.

April 30

If someone wants to wallow in self pity, let him. You are not asked to test the man but to test yourself. You are not asked to prove it to another, just yourself.

May

Stop looking for the Master to come;
he is with you always.

1 May

There is no greater influx of Spirit into a Blake, into a Shakespeare, into an Einstein, into you, than your own wonderful human imagination, for there is nothing greater. There is only one Spirit in man and the Universe!

2 May

We are all careless and often think a problem will take care of itself, but it will not. The power to change anything will lie dormant unless we operate it, as Imagination does not operate itself.

3 May

There is no stopping the man who can think *from* the end. Nothing can stop him.

May 4

There can be no objectified expression unless there is first a subjective impression.

May 5

We have already obtained it. It may appear tonight, depending upon what seed you planted.

May 6

Your attention is the sap of life which sustains the expression of your life.

7 May

Education is not accomplished by putting something into man; its purpose is to draw out of man the wisdom which is latent within him.

8 May

If it is unlovely, you are its cause. If it is lovely, you are its cause.

9 May

Because life molds the outer world to reflect the inner arrangement of our minds, there is no way of bringing about the outer perfection we seek other than by the transformation of ourselves.

May 10

You have the power to change your present and your future by writing a glorious tale about yourself and those you love.

May 11

An assumption builds a bridge of incidents that lead inevitably to the fulfilment of itself.

May 12

The habit of seeing only that which our senses permit, renders us totally blind to what we otherwise could see.

13 May

Imagination it seems will do nothing that we wish until we enter into the image of the wish fulfilled.

14 May

The range of imagining is such that I must confess that I do not know what limits, if any, there are to its ability to create reality.

15 May

If you are dissatisfied with your present expression of life, then you must be born again.

May 16

Through your ability to think and feel you have dominion over all creation.

May 17

There is no transforming power in time, only transformation of the moment.

May 18

You must know what you want before you can ask for it.

19 May

We live in a wonderful world, thinking we are going to change things, but nothing is changed on the outside. They can only be changed from within

20 May

You know, money doesn't care who owns it.

21 May

Not facts–but dreams of fancy shape our lives.

May 22

All is consciousness modified by belief.

May 23

You cannot grow and not outgrow in this world. To outgrow is to die. You die to one state and move into another state.

May 24

If man's concept of himself were different, everything in his world would be different. His concept of himself being what it is, everything in his world must be as it is.

25 May

Through his power to imagine and feel and his freedom to choose the idea he will entertain, man has control over creation.

26 May

You think you can imagine and not affect others? Everyone will in some way be influenced by your pattern.

27 May

The game of life is won by those who compare their thoughts and feelings within to what appears on the outside. And the game is lost by those who do not recognize this law.

May 28

The reason you function as you do today is because you are a creature of habit, and habit blinds you to what you desire to see. Habit acts as a compelling force, but it is not a law!

May 29

Learn to forgive everyone in this world. They are all playing their parts.

May 30

Right now you are playing a part. If you don't like it you can change it. You could play the part of a man wealthier than you were twenty-four hours ago. It's only a part for you to play, if you desire it.

31 May

You do not have to be rich to be happy but you must be imaginative! You could have great wealth and be afraid of tomorrow's needs, or have nothing and travel the world over, for all things exist in your own wonderful human imagination.

June

Not one thing is out of order.

1 June

No one can lose what he has save by detachment from the state where the things experienced have their natural life.

2 June

We can think about something forever and never see it in our world, but once let us feel its reality, and we are bound to encounter it. The more intensely we feel, the sooner we will encounter it.

3 June

The undisciplined mind finds it difficult to assume a state which is denied by the senses.

June 4

Deny it if you will, it still remains a fact that consciousness is the only reality and things but mirror that which you are conscious of being.

June 5

What you do not want done unto you, do not feel that it is done unto you or another.

June 6

If you believe that every thought produces what it implies, then stop a negative, undesirable thought, and change the record by putting on a new one.

7 June

You are inwardly talking every moment in time. What are you saying?

8 June

Feeling is the secret of creation.

9 June

If, while riding the bus, driving the car, sitting at home, or standing at a bar, you hear a remark and react by moving on the inside, that remark will fulfil itself in what your life becomes. This principle sets you free, if you are willing to assume its responsibility.

June 10

Make believe—great wonders are possible.

June 11

The moment you look back at your former state, you re-enter it, as all states exist preserved in your imagination and ready for occupancy.

June 12

To become attentive to a former state is to return to that condition.

13 June

To attempt to change the world before we change our concept of ourselves is to struggle against the nature of things.

14 June

Good or evil, a blessing or a curse, it is entirely up to you.

15 June

Don't take anything lightly. You are creating morning, noon and night.

June 16

When we walk by sight, we know our way by objects which our eyes see. When we walk by faith we order our life by scenes and actions which only imagination sees.

June 17

By disciplining your thoughts, you rise from the sleep of unawareness, and become aware of what you want to imagine. Then the world will change to conform to the change in you.

June 18

Dream lovely dreams, for you can realize everything if you are willing to imagine that you have them now.

19 June

Man does not command things to appear by his words, which are, more often than not, a confession of his doubts and fears. Decreeing is ever done in consciousness.

20 June

When man discovers that life is a play which he, himself, is consciously or unconsciously writing, he will cease from the blind, self-torture of executing judgement upon others.

21 June

Life, like music, can by a new setting turn all its discords into harmonies.

June 22

All we have to do is widen, a little bit, our concept of causality to forgive all in the world, to excuse everything in the world, for they are all playing their parts.

June 23

Imagination creates, conserves and transforms.

June 24

The confident expectation of a cure does that which no medical treatment can accomplish.

25 June

To feel *I will be* is to confess *I am not*; *I am* is stronger than *I am not*.

26 June

Your reactions to life define you, and as long as they remain as they are, your life will stay the same.

27 June

No one to change but self.

June 28

It's entirely up to you what you think. If you want to hate someone, you can augment it through intensity and persistence. The same thing is true if you want to love someone; for your human imagination is the only God you will ever know.

June 29

Knowing all things are possible to him who believes, can you persuade yourself that, although your reason and senses deny it, your assumption will make it so?

June 30

A new idea will not become part of your common currency of thought until it has been repeated over and over and you begin to live by it.

July

A change of feeling is a change of destiny.

1 July

Knowing what to do is not enough. You, imagination's operant power, must be willing to assume that things are as you desire them to be before they can ever come to pass.

2 July

Every state is already there as "mere possibility" as long as you think *of* it, but is overpoweringly real when you think *from* it.

3 July

The fact is, you are creating your destiny every moment, whether you know it or not.

July 4

Your feelings create the pattern from which your world is fashioned, and a change of feeling is a change of pattern.

July 5

Man's ignorance of the working of the law does not excuse him nor save him from the results.

July 6

It's the inner speech that is frozen in the world about us

7 July

Positive thoughts produce positive effects.

8 July

Whatever state has your attention holds your life.

9 July

Prayer is not petition; prayer is giving thanks. You don't get down on your knees and petition anyone outside of yourself. There is no intermediary between yourself and Self.

July 10

Do not look to another as the cause of your misfortune. If you are perceiving a thing, it is penetrating your brain; therefore it exists in you.

July 11

Life is a game and, like all games, it has its aims and its rules.

July 12

Do not limit yourself to the past.

13 July

Remember, there is no such thing as a powerful fate to which you must bow, nor do you have to accept life on the basis of the world without. Turn to self.

14 July

Do not limit yourself by anything that is now happening, no matter what it is.

15 July

When you imagine seeing the world as you desire it to be and are inspired as to its truth, it doesn't matter what anyone else thinks.

July 16

One seed will grow overnight while other seeds take a little longer, but each has its own appointed hour.

July 17

To remove the veil of the senses we do not employ great effort; the objective world vanishes by turning our attention away from it.

July 18

There can be no outer change until there is first an inner change.

19 July

It hardly ever crosses our minds that this world might be different in essence from what common sense tells us it so obviously is.

20 July

If you attempt to change the world before you change your attitude towards it, your struggle will be in vain.

21 July

Don't question how it can be done; simply feel that you have it.

July 22

To be realized, the wish must be felt as a state that *is* rather than a state that *is not*.

July 23

Not until the image is entered does the event burst upon the world.

July 24

Don't get in the habit of judging and criticizing, seeing only unlovely things. You have a life—live it nobly.

25 July

At every moment of your life you have the choice of several futures.

26 July

When you imagine for another, you are really giving it to yourself, as there is no other. The whole vast world is only yourself pushed out.

27 July

Governments are not something that is forecast upon the world; you and I by our change of states make the government. Want to change the government? Change yourself.

July 28

You can be anything you want to be, for you are going to be what you are imagining anyway. As man imagines, he lives! Morning, noon, and night you can't stop imagining.

July 29

A concert pianist must constantly practice for if he does not and he is called upon to give a concert he would not be ready. You must practice the art of imagining day after day so that when you are faced with a problem you will not put it aside, but will do something about it.

July 30

It is not what you want that you attract; you attract what you believe to be true.

31 July

When you see a disturbance in your world you may question why, but it appeared because you did not control your imagination. You may enjoy carrying on arguments with your children, your parents, or friends, from premises that are stupid and need not be; but if you know that all things must come to pass, why are you doing it?

August

Everything depends on your concept
of yourself.

1 August

Never envy the good fortune of another, simply appropriate your own.

2 August

Your state of consciousness creates the conditions of your life, rather than the conditions creating your state of consciousness.

3 August

You imagined yourself into the state you are now occupying, and you can imagine yourself into any state you desire to express. No outside deity moved you into the state of misery you are now expressing; you did it yourself because you forgot who you are.

August 4

The whole vast world is yourself pushed out.

August 5

Become aware of the thoughts you are thinking and you will know a more pleasant life. It makes no difference what others do; plant loving, kind thoughts and you will be blessed in the doing.

August 6

To assume the feeling of satisfaction is to call conditions into being which will mirror satisfaction.

7 August

The secret of creation is imagining.

8 August

The time it takes your assumption to become fact, your desire to be fulfilled, is directly proportionate to the naturalness of your feeling of already being what you want to be—of already having what you desire.

9 August

Disregard appearances and feel that things are as you wish them to be.

August 10

All phenomena are formed of the same substance vibrating at different rates.

August 11

Everything we do, unaccompanied by a change of consciousness, is but futile readjustment of surfaces.

August 12

I assume that feeling of the wish fulfilled and I drench myself with that feeling. Then I open my eyes and the world denies it. It doesn't really matter. Let me remain faithful to that end and it will come to pass.

13 August

The future must become the present in the imagination of the one who would wisely and consciously create circumstances.

14 August

It is imagination which makes one a leader while the lack of it makes one a follower.

15 August

Perhaps another has injured you or caused you grief. It doesn't matter what has been done, when you know this law you can forgive anyone by rearranging the structure of your mind and set him free by imagining it never happened!

August 16

By the power of imagination all men, certainly imaginative men, are forever casting forth enchantments, and all men, especially unimaginative men, are continually passing under their power.

August 17

Believing is simply living in the feeling of actually being the state imagined—by assuming the consciousness of being the state desired.

August 18

You can become self-persuaded of anything, and if you do, it will project itself on your screen of space.

19 August

If you are in debt, what is the solution? That you win the lottery or an uncle dies and leaves you his fortune? No! The end is that you are debt-free. How would you feel if all of your bills were paid? Assume that feeling and let imagination harden that feeling into a fact!

20 August

You are infinitely greater than you could ever conceive yourself to be.

21 August

Always imagine and expect the best.

August 22

At this moment you are aware of being, but you are also aware of being someone. This someone is the veil that hides the being you really are.

August 23

Just because a thing is unpleasant, don't discard it, revise it.

August 24

It is your imagination which forms the light, makes the good, and creates the evil, and there is no other God.

25 August

Unless the individual imagines himself someone else, or somewhere else, the present conditions and circumstances of his life will continue in being and his problems recur, for all events renew themselves from his constant images.

26 August

To protest against anything which happens to us is to protest against the law of our being and our rulership over our own destiny.

27 August

It is our conception of ourselves which frees or constrains us.

August 28

By our imagination we have created this dream of life, and by our imagination we will re-enter that external world of light, becoming that which we were before we imagined the world

August 29

That which you dislike will change only to the degree that you change your attitude towards it. Until you do, it cannot change for the dislike is coming from within you.

August 30

Man rates wealth in a way that bears no relation to real values.

.

31 August

Do not blame another for the events in your life. There is no one you can turn to as its cause, and don't let anyone blame you, as they are creating their own world by what they are imagining.

September

Nothing is independent of your perception.

1 September

To know what to do is not the same as doing it.

2 September

Deny the evidence of the senses, and assume the feeling of the wish fulfilled.

3 September

What the world looks like depends entirely on where man is when he makes his observation.

September 4

As surely as the day follows the night, any attribute, consciously claimed, will manifest itself.

September 5

You need no priest, no so called healer; you need nothing on the outside; it's all within Self.

September 6

What you are inwardly saying and doing is far more important than what you outwardly know or express.

7 September

The man in the state of wealth may have lots of money, but he is the same being, in a spiritual sense, as the man who is poor. The only difference is that the poor man does not know he can leave the state of poverty.

8 September

When you change your attitude towards another, he must change his attitude towards you.

9 September

You never attract that which you want but always that which you are.

September 10

It is for us to assemble the images of happy outcome and then keep from interfering. The event must not be forced but allowed to happen.

September 11

The visible world of itself can do nothing; it only bears record of its creator, the subjective state.

September 12

The moment you accept the wish as an accomplished fact the subconscious finds means for its realization.

13 September

Whatever is awake within your consciousness, you are.

14 September

Man turns outward in his search for truth but the essential thing is to look within.

15 September

The ideal is always waiting to be incarnated, but unless we ourselves offer the ideal to the Lord, our consciousness, by assuming that we are already that which we seek to embody, it is incapable of birth.

September 16

A man's enemies are those of his own household which is everything he accepts as true.

September 17

Do not allow anyone to act as an intermediary between you and your God, for He is within you!

September 18

Accept awareness as your way of life, and you will find a freedom you have never known before. You will become aware of the fact that everyone and everything is yourself pushed out.

19 September

However we toil or struggle, we can receive no more than our assumptions affirm.

20 September

Take no one and dethrone him, but do not give him the power that rightfully belongs to God.

21 September

Man transmits ideas to the subconscious through his feelings.

September 22

There is only one substance in the world. Our scientists call it energy while scripture defines it as consciousness.

September 23

I would like to give you an immense belief in miracles, but a miracle is only the name given by those who have no knowledge of the power and function of imagination to the works of imagination.

September 24

Here is the secret. Man is all imagination, and God is man and exists in us and we in Him.

25 September

Do not be concerned as to how, when, or where—only the end.

26 September

We create by faith, and faith is belief in the thing not yet seen.

27 September

Listen closely to your invisible thoughts. What do you hear? What are your words implying? That is their potency.

September 28

Things wither and die through indifference. They are kept alive through attention.

September 29

Imagination is itself indestructible. Therein lies the horror of its misuse.

September 30

There is no opponent in the game of life; there is only the goal.

October

Every man's words are his judge.

1 October

Nothing stands between man and the fulfilment of his dream but facts. And facts are the creations of imagining. If man changes his imagining, he will change the facts.

2 October

You may know the law from A to Z, but knowing is not enough. Knowledge must be acted upon.

3 October

You are not fated to become wise or foolish, rich or poor.

October 4

A controlled imagination and steadied attention, firmly and repeatedly focused on the idea to be realized, is the beginning of all magical operations.

October 5

The present moment is all important, for it is only in the present moment that our assumptions can be controlled.

October 6

My own disappointments in my world led up to what I am doing today.

7 October

Most of us don't remember and when we are confronted with our own harvest, we deny it's our harvest.

8 October

It cannot be stated too often that consciousness is the one and only reality, for this is the truth that sets man free.

9 October

You do not deny a thing by saying it does not exist. Rather you put feeling into it by recognizing it, and what you recognize as true, is true to you, be it good, bad or indifferent.

October 10

If this world is reality I cannot change it; but if I am its reality, I can change my world relative to myself. I can imagine a desire fulfilled and watch it come to pass in my outer world.

October 11

I am told I am not discriminating enough, for I can find nothing to condemn.

October 12

Nothing begins except in the imagination of man.

13 October

We must imagine we are what we would like to be. We must play it in imagination first—not as a spectator—as an actor.

14 October

It is the height of folly to expect changes to come about by the mere passage of time.

15 October

Beliefs invariably awaken what they affirm.

October 16

When man solves the mystery of imagining, he will have discovered the secret of causation, and that is: Imagining creates reality.

October 17

Only by observing your own consciousness can you discover the cause of what is happening to you.

October 18

Whether the belief pertains to self or another does not matter, for the believer is defined by the sum total of his beliefs or subconscious assumptions.

19 October

All imaginative men and women are forever casting for the enchantments, and all passive men and women, who have no powerful imaginative lives, are continually passing under the spell of their power.

20 October

Your state of awareness, like a magnet, attracts life.

21 October

Experience convinces me that the moment I have revised and relived will not recede into my past, it will advance into my future to confront me as I have revised it.

October 22

Do not concern yourself as to how it is going to happen; simply go to the end.

October 23

It is your belief in a thing not the thing itself that aids you.

October 24

To be joyful for another is to bless ourselves as well as him.

25 October

Life on earth is a training ground for image making. If you use only the molds which your senses dictate, there will be no change in your life.

26 October

If you know what you want in this world you can get it.

27 October

Realization of your wish is accomplished by assuming the feeling of the wish fulfilled.

October 28

You can go any place in this world if you don't put barriers on yourself. It's entirely up to you.

October 29

Turn from what is to what ought to be.

October 30

Man must firmly come to believe that reality lies within him and not without.

31 October

I urge everyone to think of time as precious!
Use each and every moment to plant a seed of
thought you want to experience. Then, when
your thoughtful seed is harvested, remember
the moment of planting; for every natural
effect has a spiritual cause which happens the
moment you dare to assume your desire is
real.

November

The mood decides your fortune.

1 November

Claim you are as free as the wind! Live nobly in your imagination. Dwell upon all the lovely things in life for yourself and others, as there is no other.

2 November

Man becomes what he imagines. He has a self determined history.

3 November

You don't have to "pull strings" to get what you want, all you need do is walk in the consciousness of already having it.

November 4

The world is a mirror wherein everyone sees himself reflected.

November 5

If you think something terrible is going to happen, rub it out of your mind. There is no plot to destroy you as an individual, race, or nation.

November 6

A change of attitude is a change of position on the playing field of life.

7 November

No man has too little imagination, but few men have disciplined their imagination.

8 November

The world in which we live is a world of imagination, and man—through his imaginal activities—creates the realities and the circumstances of life; this he does either knowingly or unknowingly.

9 November

Receiving a gift does not mean that we are going to use it wisely. But everyone has the gift and the world simply reflects the use of that gift.

November 10

The world is our clay; our Imagination is the Potter.

November 11

All that you believe God to be, you are; but you will never know this to be true until you stop claiming it of another, and recognize this seeming other to be yourself.

November 12

If you had a different concept of yourself, everything would be different.

13 November

To think from the end; to enact the end, is to create reality.

14 November

By intensity of hatred we create in ourselves the character we imagine in our enemies.

15 November

It's never too late to start if you know who God is. God is your own Wonderful Human Imagination.

November 16

Plant a good seed or a bad seed; it's entirely up to you.

November 17

The thieves who rob you are your own false beliefs.

November 18

What would you think and say and do were you already the one you want to be?

19 November

Consciousness is the one and only reality.

20 November

As mental arguments produce conflicts, so happy mental conversations produce corresponding visible states of good tidings.

21 November

The subconscious is what a man is. The conscious is what a man knows.

November 22

Dream the most glorious, noble dreams and then rest relative to the state you judge perfect.

November 23

It is the frequency, the habitual occupancy, that is the secret of success. The more often we do it, the more natural it is.

November 24

The only work you are called upon to do is work on yourself.

25 November

Man attracts what he *is*.

26 November

When someone comes into your world, don't discard him by turning your back because he is ill, financially troubled, or not successful in his own eyes. Rather, see his desire as clay in your imaginal hands. Take that same vessel (person) and rework him into another state as it seems good to you to do.

27 November

Believing and being are one.

November 28

You cannot fail unless you fail to convince yourself of the reality of your wish.

November 29

Learn to consciously play this game of life, for you are unconsciously playing it every day.

November 30

What we desire does not lie in the future but in ourselves at this very moment.

December

Dreams are realized not by the rich,
but by imagination.

1 December

The state you would transmit to another can be transmitted only if it is believed by you. Therefore, to give is to receive.

2 December

When you can persuade yourself 100% that you are successful, success is yours! You must become so intense that you completely forget it was only a desire. You must tame the wild, new state you have entered until its naturalness causes you to forget all else.

3 December

It is only what is done *now* that counts.

December 4

People have a habit of slighting the importance of simple things. Being creatures of habit, we are slow to relinquish previous concepts and the things we formerly lived by still influence our behaviour.

December 5

You and God are one and undivided

December 6

All that you could ever desire is already present and only waits to be matched by your beliefs.

7 December

Imagine better than the best you know, and create a better world for yourself and others.

8 December

As an individual, you move and live in time, but your true being is in eternity.

9 December

Never accept anything as true and final unless it conforms to the ideal you desire to embody within your world.

December 10

It is a marvellous thing to find that you can imagine yourself into the state of your fulfilled desire and escape from the jails which ignorance built.

December 11

As soon as we succeed in transforming ourselves, the world will melt magically before our eyes and reshape itself in harmony with that which our transformation affirms.

December 12

As you imagine, so your life is going to be.

13 December

I think all happiness depends on the energy to assume the feeling of the wish fulfilled, to assume the mask of some other more perfect life.

14 December

If we remember another as we have known him, we recreate him in that image, and the past will be recognized in the present.

15 December

At every moment of our lives we have before us the choice of which of several futures we will choose.

December 16

Sin is simply knowing what to do and not doing it.

December 17

If one imagines unlovely things for another, they are going to produce them—not in the other, but in themselves.

December 18

All things are made by imagination's power.

19 December

Complacency is a curse.

20 December

It is silly to accept something simply because the church said it, or you read it in the Bible, or heard it from Neville. You must pursue the thought ceaselessly by questioning yourself.

21 December

Do not try to change people; they are only messengers telling you who you are.

December 22

If you long to transform your present life into a dream of what might well be, you need but imagine that you are already what you want to be and to feel the way you would expect to feel under such circumstances.

December 23

Everything is a thought before it becomes a thing.

December 24

If you have a goal you can attain it. You can attain it by the use of your own wonderful human imagination.

25 December

Prayer is the master key. A key may fit one door of a house, but when it fits all doors it may well claim to be a master key. Such and no less a key is prayer to all earthly problems.

26 December

To play the game of life successfully, we must become aware of our every mental activity.

27 December

Free will actually means freedom to select any idea you desire.

December 28

People feeling poor attract poverty, not knowing that if they felt rich they would attract wealth.

December 29

There is a wide difference between the will to resist an activity and the decision to change it. He who changes an activity acts; whereas he who resists an activity, reacts. One creates, the other perpetuates.

December 30

Love and hate have a magical transforming power, and we grow through their exercise into the likeness of what we contemplate.

31 December

If you want something, you can have it, but you must be willing to give up what you are now in order to be what you want to be. That is the only price you pay. No sacrifice is required outside of giving up the state in which you find yourself and moving into the state where you want to be, for they are only states.

Have you lived this life of yours
in such a way
that you desire to live it again?

Neville